A PAINTER'S NIGHT JOURNAL

poems by

Meg Lindsay

Finishing Line Press
Georgetown, Kentucky

A PAINTER'S NIGHT JOURNAL

for Gary, love of my life and witness to the vicissitudes of creating
for Nick, whose single-minded focus inspires
for Julia, her wide-ranging erudition and insights

Copyright © 2016 by Meg Lindsay
ISBN 978-1-63534-051-8 First Edition
All rights reserved under International and Pan-American Copyright Conventions.
No part of this book may be reproduced in any manner whatsoever without written permission from the publisher, except in the case of brief quotations embodied in critical articles and reviews.

ACKNOWLEDGMENTS

Grateful acknowledgment is given to the editors of the following publications in which these poems first appeared, some in slightly different versions:
Salamander: "Watching the Wall Hangings in the Aldrich Museum of Contemporary Art"
The Westchester Review: "Ask," "Jennifer Bartlett's Gardens"

Publisher: Leah Maines

Editor: Christen Kincaid

Cover Art: Meg Lindsay

Author Photo: Roy Weinstein, Roy Weinstein Photography

Cover Design: Elizabeth Maines

Printed in the USA on acid-free paper.
Order online: www.finishinglinepress.com
       also available on amazon.com

Author inquiries and mail orders:
Finishing Line Press
P. O. Box 1626
Georgetown, Kentucky 40324
U. S. A.

Table of Contents

Nature Morte (for Morandi) 1
Blue Beach Umbrellas 2
Ask 3
Painting Sheep 4
Tuscany 6
Turkish Threads 7
Jennifer Bartlett's Gardens 10
Clouds 11
Palette 12
Diminish 13
Painting in Lake Placid 14
Sketching 17
39 Canvasses/how to hang an exhibition 18
The Smaller Format 19
The Painter in Home Depot 20
Literalist 22
Search 24
Unmapped 25
Problem of Accrual 30
Watching the Wall Hangings in the Aldrich Museum 31
Perseverance 32
Mother/Unframed 34
The End of Light 36

*Painting is poetry that is seen rather than felt,
and poetry is painting that is felt
rather than seen.*

—Leonardo da Vinci

NATURE MORTE
(for Morandi)

Where is that squattish bottle, azure blue,
the blue of Turkey, from the time of my handsome, stubborn
Turkish lover?
A pomegranate shape,
its surface hacked with odd facets.

Did this husband drop that bottle too and not mention it,
hoping I'd forget? Or is it gone
like my phone number from my mother's mind.

I am sick of bottles.
I've done them before.
Flowers are an excuse for texture and light
but I will do pears: the reddish or the green
of early Sienna's terre verte
      —the Bosc or Anjou.

I struggle with the shapes
and echoes of blackbirds or a Brazilian river or two.
It only works when you're mad.
A twist of the palette knife flicks a dollop of slick ivory black.

See the late afternoon light just before the sun turns blood red,
noiselessly lisp across the lumpy fruit
defined by the shadows between.

BLUE BEACH UMBRELLAS

why aren't I painting you?

bright
like peaked
striped, Seuss hats

cloths collapsed, their ends
poked up
at the grey/blue (sky) dome
with its cobalt anvil thunderheads

in the sticky August air

sand
the color
of sand

ASK

Sometimes I forget the camera, forget
that the late afternoon sun can mix with the earth's warmed dust,
as it soaks back up from the fields.
We are driving from his parents' camp on the Tug Hill Plateau,
flat and dull until I start to see
the odd checkerboard patterns of meadow
fan out in palest milky golds.
I want to stop, be free of our car,
flee into the fields, feel the light, capture the light,
inhale it, splay it across the soft resist of a stretched, virgin linen—
in slick varnish shine through the wet
with the glow of russet and Naples yellow.
We are driving fast.
My husband is talking about
what he wants to tell his boss
and an old sheep, barely white, cream,
stands alone by a bent stub of a tree,
munching, mouth working around, watching
as we barrel along.
We are supposed to be in Lake Placid before dark
and it will be tight
and the light is a way I have never seen before.
I say his name and I am aching inside,
not knowing why,
as he shifts his foot to press the brake,
it is so hard to ask.

PAINTING SHEEP

I sketch, stand with my wire-bound pad
and Blackwing pencils, the lead soft and dark.
My hand swoops round the bulbous shapes,
jabs little sharp strokes for the knobby knees
and that odd patch of wool sticking straight up
on top of the head, ragged
so my pencil zigzags to chase it between floppy ears.
Munching, working, round small mouths.
Sunflowers in August salt the fields orange.

Why is it so hard to make my husband stop the car?
Is it my husband? He always stops if I ask.

Where the trail dips toward the base of Cascade
a stream of glassy water magnifies the glacially rounded stones.
I like to hike.
I like to use my body
but my husband's always ahead with his book on philosophy, waiting
on a rock, like a mountain goat, watching me catch up
while I place the sole of my boot
alongside, not across the thick roots,
step after step
remembering the sprained ankles,
the scent of my sweat attracting small black flies.

What if I stop for a moment? The trees are scarred
when the wind pulls away their mask.

The sheep are far out in closed pastures.
Dozens—puffy, dirty brown sheep
shag across lumpy fields on skinny stick legs.
I knock on the one weathered house.
An old man gets a young man with dark hair,
the one who breeds the blackface sheep. With his wife
we three walk in the fields hidden from the road.

She smiles but is missing teeth
and the lines in her face make me look away.
He says she is Italian.
In their gardens when I ask about strawberries
he snorts about frosts in August:
only potatoes and roots grow this far north
but I see his wife's dahlias, snapdragons, zinnias
dancing, wind-tossed, a froth of pink.

*Take a stand. Stand on my own. Instead, I feel a student again
caught in a slow, dry task.*

My fingers too numb to sketch,
thick paper prints grind out of my Polaroid—
in black mists bright eyes and spindly legs take shape.
Shaggy coats from a distance that look like great capes,
close up are matted and stained.
Under tail flaps, clots of dung and mud.

*In a creased photo a grimace mars my mother's face,
a cigarette smoking from between her lacquered fingertips.*

Nothing moves in the fields.
Gone the barn's crude wooden doors that kept foxes out.
Instead thick Thermopane reflects a grey sky,
white sale stickers stuck on the glass.
I'd meant to ask the farmer
about the one sheep that never moved off, her back legs stiff.
Clotted wool hung down her matt black face,
blocked her dull yellow eye.
She turned her head slightly, as if to see.

TUSCANY

Today so hot we bagged it, missed
the Museum of Medieval Atrocities.

These swallows are not thrilled
to see my shoulders still in their window

whose screenless shutters spread open
to the dusty trapezoids of grape fields.

Stick-like trunks of cypress trees
muffle the whining scooters. A screech

of swallow—black wings draping
a pale belly—swoops by my head.

Like tiny guards, they eye me
from their crusted turf—a roof of rows
of curved, bled terra cotta tiles.

These swallows' wingtips droop, like those
Fra Angelico painted,
    "The Annunciation"
 —a saintly sway, the ends of angel wings—
the gloss of mottled blades.

TURKISH THREADS

I.
This pink is not a pink, is a brown
but is pink next to the apple green;
both middle tones
   —indistinguishable as in a black and white photograph—
invite.

A contemporary design: clean, small triangles,
flat wedge shapes each with 3 points,
each either bright apple green or a much darker olive
floats in the ground of brown.

In this Istanbul hotel wall to wall
   is not the traditional Hajji Baba Kilim
and so *is*
a Turkish rug.

II.
My son and daughter-in-law talk of their baby
due in 4 months.
They visit day care centers.
My son racks his brain to ask the right trick question:
   do they hold the babies when no one's looking?
How did we assess my mother's Alzheimer's ward?
No lucid witnesses.

III.
The brown-that-becomes-the-pink-because-of-apple-green
calls for me to pick up a brush to slide slick oil paint
into the caches of rough canvas,
calls to me to reflect. Don't the greens
reflect
a relationship of greens?
The apple green is not enough:
its tone too similar to pink–brown,
needs the darker olive,
a darker side to set off the relationship of the other two.

IV.
My son and daughter-in-law read books on child development.
A light spot on the sonogram shows it's a boy,
 and if his mother drinks caffeinated tea, his kicking keeps her awake.
Thirty two years ago my son, unborn,
seemed to wedge his feet on the underside of my ribs to push off
in a gusty amniotic swim.

V.
A Hungarian with the longest hands gives birth to me in colors
 —a slow spiral.
A sculptor, he sculpts me in shapes and their shadows
which set them off:
 gradation of shadow, reflected
within the larger shadow.
He leads me into a painting, points out a sneaky pink,
pink painted as half a creamy moon.

I'd fought pink,
round little collars on cotton dresses with beaded smocking.
At five I knew already my mother's path of dark denial
 —her sudden tears.

My teacher's pink glows in oil next to
what I learn to be sap green, a translucent olive color, slippery,
squeezed out from crumpling metal tubes,
 full-bodied paint forced out.

Pink is just a color:
 what color is it next to?

VI.
I'd thought my days of child-raising were over: the ledger's shut,
 its lessons absorbed
but now it starts again—slumbering dragons.

My son worries I won't spend enough time with his child.
A friend says her son feels his ancient grudges heal
when he sees her singing to his baby.
My husband and my son and daughter-in-law,
    their voices and concern rise
with theories of the consequences
of different civilizations' child-bearing policies.
The theories soothe
as this thing swells, kicks, swims along,
bigger and bigger in her belly.

VII.
How to create the ground that subtly vibrates plain brown into pink?
How to make a triad, not the solution but the complement,
the embrace. The bigger holding,
the separate parts never lost but enveloped, whole and visible.

VIII.
Instead of saying *I love you* my husband and I have a fight.
He goes to a separate bed because he will run a marathon
next morning before a ten day business trip.
But I want to feel his warmth.

Instead of saying *I miss you*, I ask him to take towels or
he'll sweat all over the upholstery in our car.

I ask my friend *why am I still with my husband after 17 years?*
She says *maybe you love him.*
What if it's not enough?

My husband says loving is not enough,
is only the part.

JENNIFER BARTLETT'S GARDENS

I let the oversized art book fall open
and grumble, "I've painted a garden or two."
Hers has a statue—a girl, milky, alone
    nestled in greens
  at the far end of a rectangular pool.
Her brush has smudged the surrounding blacks.

I flip a couple of pages.
The pool again but the figure has shrunk,
    tiny at the bottom of tree spires.
 Those blues (*you know*
she took a fat wet brush
and laid it on the bristled side, soft sable,
let it leach into the toothy stock forever, rolled
the sodden, soggy brush—
raw, rough blues,
paper whites showing raggedly through—
  cacophony beyond the gardened trees).

On the slip case flap, a small photograph
blurred in black and white of the artist's face.

At the back of the book at the end of the pool
our girl (that face again)—
    above, viridians
  and rose shards flutter
off into endless cerulean,
her body in its pool of white paper
defined by negative space.

CLOUDS

Today I will paint cloud patterns.
Not clouds. Their patterns.
Not owls. Not cows.
I've moved on
from *why*,
when I forgot to wonder
what patterns exist
in clouds at all,
vanished when not
locked down
on a canvas.

PALETTE

1. The Yellow Sock with the Blue

Painters wear their palettes—
look to their socks, one citron yellow,
the other a cerulean blue.

A room of writers is a room of grey wrens—
listen for the color in their songs,
don't look at their socks.

Writers are sandpipers chasing the tide.
They wet their feet, dart back to pick over what's shining.
What's that belly up? in the receding waters.

II. Metaphor

A painting is glue and dirt on cloth.
A poem is scratchings on a sheet of paper.
Or is it sounds in the night?

To write about a spider,
write about the rock
around which it spins its web.

III. Boredom is a high

you escape
as emptiness, its mistaken sister.
Boredom is the white light that holds creation
but you see only fog
stirred by your agitations
and forget what needs to be said.

DIMINISH

Unwilling to live from memory,
unwilling to see only to record,
I stop trying to copy the sky
(that blue? cerulean?)
as if anyone could copy the sky
and stop trying
(maybe a squeeze of ultramarine?)
to memorize
that slash of late afternoon light
across your cheek,
stop making note how it fades
into black
so close to your ear,
so afraid you might turn
to speak
and lose the light,
diminish
what is there.

PAINTING IN LAKE PLACID

I.
Looking at the tall
pine trees with their fluffy green boughs
and snatches of cerulean sky poking through,
I remember paintings of 19th century artists
on craggy cliffs at easels
perched under jaunty umbrellas bleached by the sun.
I paint in my head,
feeling the smudge and shmush of mixed oils
in my mind, feeling my way along the bough
as with a smaller brush,
slipping the branch darkly
among…
and that is when I
stopped painting,
when what I saw
ceased to be the rich
varieties of the external world but instead
became only the excuse
for the seductive transfer onto canvas,
the shift into a hand
manipulating a brush.
A catapult.
A loss of connection.

II.
I'd become a scavenger not unlike
the raptors I'd painted
with their weightless hollow bones,
owls with their reputation for *wise*,
but stupidest of beasts,
fluffing feathers to scare away a foe,
light as air except for
beak and talons
to shred the just dead flesh—

in attempts to sustain new life
to respond to their babies' demanding beaks, squeakings
and shiverings, yearning to survive.

III.
I stop painting for a while,
feel illegitimate.
The delusion of illusion
more ominous than empty,
fear not of the inner
but of the shift—
brief flicker of color bent to spontaneous vision
through initiating will.

IV.
But how seductive is paint.
The once empty canvas primed a warm white,
invites staining with diluted color, becomes heavier
with the spreading splatters and drips.
The smooth steady sweep of a palette knife
loaded with fat dollops of oily
mixed alizarin, smears slick translucent sap green
or whacks with a smudge of a subdued madder red.
The sharp flick and sprang of the knife's rounded metal tip
as it catches and scratches and rasps,
its long edge scraping down the crags
of dried underpainting built up,
blended hints of orange and ochre
peaking evocatively through the blue,
until the thing comes
to be seen in itself.

V.
Older, grounded in the supposed tricks
of life and mind,
more healed, re-embrace
the interactions
that result
on the canvas,
an implied contract,
like each painting, uniquely signed and owned.
In the end, what is left.

SKETCHING

In the mottled shade
odd little bugs flit about
a label that says
screech owl.
Puffed up over her talons
clutched to her roost,
her head swivels, as she silently tracks.
Darkly quiet.
Blind with cataracts.
Old at 28.
But who can tell?
Mottled feathers
instead of wrinkled skin.
And the caged, male cormorant
black iridescent plumage in season
his jade eyes, flecked orbs
ringed with cerulean dots,
the slender beak patched bright orange
and, as it opens
perhaps to sing?
inside that beak, seduced,
the bright sky blue of heaven.

39 CANVASSES
how to hang an exhibition

*Each demands its fit
in an order
of universe.
An outline is an easy way out,
a map that tells too much
because I know,
although not knowing,
each will have its place*

just as I know like an itch when a canvas
needs something more, when I take a thin brush,
wetly rolled in the dripping imperfection of color,
a finalizing twist splayed in annoyance
across the contrived,
to expose a rich surprise.

*Images wink from their positions,
leaned against the gallery wall
as I go back and forth,
up the ladder
and down.*

On canvasses I have worried shapes
into illusions of depth, layered opposite colors,
abutted areas of slightly different hues,
their juxtapositions creating a line
where no line is drawn

*but exhibiting is not like painting the 39.
Hanging a show is like packing to move,
at first manageable, then overwhelmed
until the larger canvasses are hung,
until the clutter lifts.*

THE SMALLER FORMAT

I can't stand the splinters that stick my palms
after I saw strips of wood lattice for five foot frames
or the soreness from gripping the X-Acto knife
to get a bevel cut clean in an acid free mat.
Worn down with physicality.
Instead I assemble smaller box-like stretchers two inches thick,
wrapping the canvas around the sides and stapling
out of sight to the back:
smooth sides require no frame.

I used to draft my husband to wait with the car
at the 56th Street gallery service entrance while I unloaded.
No more will I hook my fingers
under unforgiving stretcher bars:
no more will I hold on tight against the wind
to anticipate the sudden gusts
that lift, flip an oversized canvas like some stiff, untethered sail
out of my grasp.
The director had rubbed her jaw, peered at my work
propped along her walls.
Startled by my trembling but with nothing to say,
I tried to remember to breathe,
barely heard for the buzz in my ears when she'd said *well, yes,
we'll keep them* and I danced back down the street.
Until I found in a year she'd never hung them at all.

A smaller surface to scrape down, this new format
is more manageable, less space
in which to dissipate, as if instead,
like increased depth of field,
a more intense focus
as I build up translucent layers of paint.

THE PAINTER IN HOME DEPOT

This polished concrete floor is hard.
I wish I'd thought
to wear softer sneakers
or could fling myself on a skate board,
zip through this empty space
looking for a box of sawtooth staples,
the aisles cavernous, banked by stocked metal shelves
arched up like the ancient densely packed trees
that line the road spiraling out
from Paris to Versailles.

Looking for sawtooths
for their bite into wood.
Looking to lengthen the life
of my old industrial stapler
although ever harder to force the pressure gun's
bolt action, too much give,
running out of the push to force the thin metal in.

This floor gets harder.
I loathe this place, the diffuse fluorescent light,
loathe being here
on concrete, heels aching,
neck bent back as I read aisle tags
posted fifteen feet high,
turn yet another corner, into yet another aisle.

Who to ask
to find a staple,
that which binds together canvas to wood,
the support of all I paint.
My heart's flutter becomes a lurch.
The floor so polished, too hard to fall on.
I picture the fat, engorged muscle of my heart, sluggish,
sloshing ventricles.
Slow. Breathe deep.

Lower my head below my heart
like I'd read.
I wrote a poem this morning
they found her under her paintings
but will it be
they find me in Aisle 3C
among plywood planks?

These flutters always pass I tell myself
and put my head further down
toward my knees,
feel the blood change course,
rush up to somewhere behind my eyes,
although it seems
there is no moment
in which this will pass,
only this moment in which I am hung, head bowed,
as if in prayer, suspended,
waiting to see,
maybe like my friend whose vision narrowed black
as she collapsed and cracked her head on a glass counter,
but this odd occasional lurch dissolves
and a man in a red apron
asks me if he can be of help.

LITERALIST

How dare he say my painting bothers him
because there are not enough legs?
Does he notice the sheep are orange?
He sits in his easy chair
and says he can't see their back legs.

I check my website
and there is a back leg for the sheep on the right
but the middle sheep's rump is obfuscated
by the front of the sheep on the left
and the canvas' left edge cuts off the rear of another.
How many legs make a sheep?
What if one were 3-legged,
attacked by wolves
and lucky to escape?

And what do I care?
They bought it. They own it.
What do I expect?
What's in a number?
4 legs or 3 or 2?
What's the tipping point,
the moment of collapse.

Was it a foggy day when the sheep
escaped the wolf?
The wolf shrouded, crept closer,
the fog embraced them,
lost even to each other,
—enveloped in mist—
except for their faces
and full front chest and 2 forelegs.
Three big sheep faces, whimsical,
their startled awareness
'captured' by that odd shadow of me,

with pen and bulky pad
in the iced mud and stinky damp,
inching slowly too close
as they melted surreptitiously away.

Scrolling through my photos
of sheep and cows and creatures
whose essence
I strained to see,
to hear in the quiet still,
beyond the idea in our heads
what we think is a sheep with four legs.
In the photos you don't see
all 4 legs, maybe the front 2
but the back 2 merge together
or, in some, a rise of grass in front
so no legs are visible at all.

Tired of explaining to people who look at a canvas
that, no, it is a cow or a duck or Aunt Matilda,
not whatever the shapes and colors trigger
in their locked-tight brains, some story,
some image reawakened, a snapshot
slumbering Jungian in dormant dreams.

Shall I send the photos as evidence?
No, I shall paint more creatures.
With lots of legs. Ten legs to a cow
as a study, like a Muybridge photo, running fast in a blur.
Maybe paint them with a quick twist of the brush
so they'll look like round baby elephants
or tadpoles or a Dumbo octopus—
newly discovered creature
of the lightless nine mile deep,
shaped oddly
with features like eyes that beg,
we might think, for midnight's duplicity.

SEARCH

I know already Jake Berthot's early paintings,
each with its massive round shape
settled in a ground of thick swirling red
but I flip open a book of his sketches
and there are, instead,
light squiggles and scratchy pen marks,
uncertainty on paper with pen,
no paint—
only minimal,
maybe subliminal?
a curved halting hook—
a smear—
even an 'A'
at the beginning but
are those letters thereafter, unintelligible
to any like me, looking at this book
where is the key
to the lock of his mind,
of his heart?
me, wondering where 'he' had gone.
Gone? If not died,
gone from the page he scribbled on.

UNMAPPED

1.
Each day I write another—
before I get out of bed before
I begin to think. A quasi dream state
of rhyme, the turn a lever back
into the not-yet-known—to become
part of a stack, from the side monolithic.

II.
Under moonlight baby turtles scratch,
hatch from their shells.
Does the salt wind tug them forward
damp crystals stuck to their craggy mouths?
Tiny flappers haphazardly flip flap,
an army rustling as it wriggles its way to the sea.

Some stumble under a laggard mother's shoveling, clumsy flippers,
pitch into that dank pit
with the sand that clumps on the newly dropped eggs
(glistening with primordial ooze),
and suffocate.

III.
No published primers.
No warning labels.

IV.
When I don't pick up the brush,
black cotton clogs my eyes and ears.

V.
That painting is clumsy:
the composition makes you tilt your head
but the awkwardness awkwardly
circles back and each tilt supports another
for some odd symmetry within the frame.

You try another medium, not the one
where your skin absorbs the sweet-smelling turpentine,
where cadmium and chrome oxide seep into your lungs.

You sit instead at a desk: a muscle spasm
spreads up your arm into your neck but you
are locked into tapping the keys as if God might speak.

VI.
Before computers—
the man who devoted his life to God,
counting the Bible's conjunctions.

VII.
Iconoclast, the New York School dribbled house paints,
fugitive pigments that lacked the proper priming.
Layers of oils drying at different rates detach, crack.

The New York School spawned a school of conservation
for wealthy titans who thought
they'd bought a stake in immortality—*art*,
found a built-in time bomb, a *fuck you*, instead.

VIII.
In the course on materials I learn
to lay oils on a primer of rabbit's skin glue.
Each layer dries at its own rate.
My steel blade scrapes down the old.

The fourteenth century Sienese were the first
to mix pigment with oil, add yellow ochre
to lead white for a warm base.

See how rose madder glows on the white,
disappears scumbled over ultramarine.

I learn my favorite sap green
—translucent, oily and dark—
is unstable, that manufacturers churn out
flashy colors to fill demand.
Just like absinthe once.

Lead white—the brightest, most permanent white—
is stocked only in art stores because teething babies
gnaw flaking house paint off window sills.

Goya goes mad and blind sucking thoughtlessly
on the tips of brushes
as visions of demons and gargoyles and
bats' wings and a monster god chewing on a headless corpse
spill onto his paper.
Poison? or
nightmares waiting for release
after decades of painting portraits of demented King Charles V.

IX.
When I complain about the lack of ventilation
the master printer scoffs
*hey, real artists love to inhale
the perfume of turps*

Latex gloves. Fans. Industrial soaps.
Removed from the touch of paint.

X.
The social worker shows me the chart of life:
birth, the development of speech, walking, abstract thought:
my mother in dementia follows the order in reverse.

XI.
Nancy Graves, (already forgotten?)
sculpted bright new plastics and resins

—bird-like creatures ten feet tall—
died of brain cancer at 55
as did Sue, a grandmother at 62
who built dollhouses by dripping encaustic.

XII.
Learning slips through like sand
trickling between my outstretched fingers
—a frittering away.

The stacked canvasses tilt against each other,
occasionally slip, poke holes into each other's
taut, stretched linen.

Try terre verte next to gold or
even a flat, matte black instead of the gloss.

How to take a letter not to make a word
but to study each carved turn,
not for the line
but the interval, the space between?

XIII.
The IRS assesses unsold paintings
as the estate to tax.
Adult children drive the prices down
as they try to sell the remains.

XIV.
Louise Nevelson smashes all the clay sculptures after her first show. Unsold.

XV.
Turtles don't use manuals.
No turtle poets.
Dig.

XVI.
Stacks of poems
monolithic, inscrutable, inaccessible
as pharaoh in his tomb.

THE PROBLEM OF ACCRUAL

The moon calls to me to paint her,
splashes her light around,

inches closer to get a better look,
her pale citron pricking its way into my dreams.

Each night she returns, creeps close to that space
between what leaves still cling among the oaks.

Her aim more direct, she hurls her diamond shafts.
My eyelids open. Bright. Impaled.

Stung, I search for your colors in my brain
but you, interest lost, slowly shift and dim.

Now, full awake in foggy morning greys,
I take a pen and pad in my warm bed

rather than, stiffly cold, descend the stairs
to face toxicity of hardening paints.

WATCHING THE WALL HANGINGS IN THE ALDRICH MUSEUM

1. A CHILD'S DRESS, BLACK THREADS SPROUT FROM THE NARROW CHEST

whiskers sail through leafless trees
the bark cracks, squeaks
encrusted beetles blow away   the new
forage on old enemies under the mottled skin
*   drying childbirth warms at first*
mutters in the mater sewing circles   snip and stitch
sepia, the dried blood of unsigned quilts I've seen before
*   as Rembrandt in a beating windmill paints rats in a cage*
*   hung on a hook until motes are the only thing he sees*

2. BLACK WOOD HANDS DRIP THREADED LETTER STRANDS DOWN THE WHITE WALL

I write   *in endless time but time runs out*
            alone, we blend our elders' stories
as I watch, the sun makes stubby shadows of my knuckles
and the phone keeps ringing   while I take my lessons
    I miss the paints that slowly kill me
    a painterly painter in a political time
a seer who gives
surreptitiously
    I want my copper hair back
"beating like a drum"
the letters curl

PERSEVERANCE

I've been painting again
and reading Pamuk's *My Name Is Red*
about book illuminators from Turkey
painting centuries ago, who avoided
looking outside—their fear of blindness.
Years ago I stopped painting outside
finding it hard to see,
dazzled by light reflected off the Hudson.
A friend, famous as a plein air colorist,
has macular degeneration; now I see the trees
in the center of his painting are white.

In Pamuk's book, the sultan,
when the painting immortalizing him
was finished, might put the illuminator to death
or blind him so he could not
immortalize anyone else. But some masters
continued to paint from memory, their fingers
searching their brushes for light.

I've been painting but one of my painter friends
has brain damage from etching decades ago, the acids,
and can't get words out anymore,
and another, her lungs damaged
from poorly ventilated fumes of turps,
struggles to breathe.
I paint in warmer months with the windows open,
my hands in green stretchy gloves bought from my dentist,
the green sticking to the sweat on my skin, puckering
in odd little creases like lines on a map

while I cannot figure out how to draw a cow.
I've drawn hundreds.
They are clunky, obstinately bulky, and inimical to a flowing line.
Do you draw one big puzzled cow
or a lot of little cows
in one big pasture
or brown cows in a green pasture
or green cows in a brown field
as the ink glistens before it sinks into
the white tooth of the sheet.

MOTHER/UNFRAMED

*When I paint your body,
do I paint what's left behind?
No, I paint the soft light
spilling onto your last bed.*

Did I irritate you when I tried to tell
you what business was like?
You bought me that suit anyway,
mahogany, thick wool weave,
snappy padded shoulders
and the long, slim skirt with a slit peeking out from a thick fold.

*When I paint your body,
What am I fed?*

Your estate's
numbers and forms
at my desk where I look
into the picture frames I took from your room:
photographs of babies, boys, young men—
my two sons growing.
I never put out pictures of my own.

*When I paint the soft light
spilling on your bed...*

You smelled of romance,
your teeth slightly crooked
when you smiled,
your glistening mink, fur deliciously cool—
when I buried my face, it tickled.
Your high heels clicking as you left, with Dad.

*When I try to paint your body,
I paint something else instead.*

We both married twice.
The first time you bought me a white leather book
to record crystal goblets and Tiffany spoons.
You ordered pale notepaper, monogrammed
with my new initials from a lead plate.
We both made long lists with our cross-looped letterings
in blue ink, now tossed together
in my attic in a box.

When I paint your body,
something unlocks.

THE END OF LIGHT

A fat orange yolk sits on top of the black horizon.

Our sun, most dazzling just before it slips away
would never set if we could chase across the vastness
of this globe,
fly due West to keep its sinking yet in sight—
   wind howls against our ears.

Instead, grounded in this body.
Aching, I rock to rest my weight
full upon the land, watch

  the shadow, the line that shifts
   —at first imperceptibly—
across this flat valley floor.
Not a line, rather an edge where two hues meet:

the creeping dark pulls up its lightless shade,
obliterates each blade of grass

as octopus ink might spread

as the painter, exhausted
toward nightfall reaches wide
to paint the broader stroke
for once, unconstrained.

Meg **Lindsay**, a painter with works juried into museum exhibitions, has always explored crossover images and patterns in her language and poems. A semi-finalist in two "Discovery"/ *The Nation Contests* and a finalist in an Inkwell competition, she has been published by *Tricycle, Pivot, Alimentum, the Connecticut River Review, Salamander, etc.* MFA Sarah Lawrence College. Paintings can be seen on her website: www.meglindsayartist.com

www.ingramcontent.com/pod-product-compliance
Lightning Source LLC
LaVergne TN
LVHW041551070426
835507LV00011B/1041